The KING ... of the peripheries

By

George Calleja

Extract of praise to George Calleja

Emmaus... in today's society

I certainly encourage anyone to read this book and to be hopeful of their own journey back to God. God bless you and thank you George.

BY: SUSAN FARRUGIA

Her Silence

This work is a well-written personal testimonial of a special relationship with the Mother of God.

BY: LAWRENCE JAKOWS

Spiritual Reflections

George Calleja's book, Spiritual Reflections, would be a great read fo r any Christian, be they young or old.

BY: BRITTANY LEWIS

Waking up the sleeping giant

I am giving this book a 4 star because I don't like to give 5 stars to re ligious books because many don't believe and have a hard time conn ecting with a book like this.

BY: P.S.WINN

Heal my wounds

Really a great book, enjoyed the insights about healing, suffering and hope.

BY: FATHER STEPHEN GEMME

Taste and see that the Lord is Good

It is a little book that is full of much wisdom.

BY: AMY

Yes... I will follow Him

What touched me the most is the story of the author's personal response of "Yes". His story proved that there is a God and He is always there for each and every one of us.

BY: IRENE KUEH

My little book of daily prayer

Find peace, love and inspiration in this great little book of heart touc hing prayers.

BY: P.S.WINN

__The Beatitudes... The Blessings from the Sermon on the Mount__

The book was helpful and positive. It is easy to read and understand. It makes you want to be a better person and be closer to Jesus. I definitely recommend that you read this book!

__*BY: ROBERT A. HUNT*__

Books published by George Calleja

'Emmaus... in today's society' – November 2020

'Come to Me' – September 2019

'Her Silence' – January 2019

'In His image' – June 2018

'Spiritual Reflections' – December 2017

'Waking up the sleeping giant' – July 2017

'Heal my Wounds' - February 2017

'The Light' - September 2016

'Taste and see that the Lord is good' - April 2016

'My Little Book of Daily Prayer' - January 2016

'The Beatitudes... the blessings from the Sermon on the Mount'
   September 2015

'Evangelization through Social Networking Sites' - June 2015

'Peace and unity in our lives' - March 2015

'Yes... I Will Follow Him' - March 2015

'Peace and unity in our lives - Volume Two' - January 2015

'Peace and unity in our lives - Volume One' - November 2014

The painting *'Your Jesus'* reproduced in the front cover of this ebook, was done by the Artist, Fabio Borg. In his own words, the interpretation of the painting *'Your Jesus'* is the following:

'In this painting my intention was to represent Jesus as a normal person - Just like one of us! He was a true God, but also a true human being. As the title of the painting conveys, I wanted to represent a personal Jesus, one who understands our situation and is there for us, just like true friends, who are there for each other.'

Title of painting: 'Your Jesus' - Medium: acrylics on canvas - Size: 40cm x 50cm

This book is dedicated to all those living in the peripheries

CONTENTS

Introduction

Mankind. Humanity. Ever since the creation of man, ever since man started to discover the earth, ever since he reached every corner of the world, man has ventured out to conquer land, to develop himself and his surroundings. Over the centuries, ever since Adam and Eve, ever since the first fall of man from his Creator, man has faced the pain of suffering which is with us till this present day.

Man has always strived to improve his life, has been attentive to safeguard himself, his family, his land, his country. History has shown us how man has ruled the world. Kingdoms were set up in every continent, ruling for power, to safeguard their land, to safeguard their wealth.

Kings have come and gone. The world has seen different kings across the globe. Kings whose life is known for their good deeds to mankind, other kings who brought destruction to their kingdom.

The world has evolved, has changed. Kings are not as powerful as they used to be. Kings are much less numerous today, having less powers, because the world has developed its political systems, where nowadays Presidents and Prime Ministers have the duty of leading their countries. But still the world talks about kings. Nowadays it is more common to talk about the king of rock 'n roll, the king of football, the king of boxing, with full admiration of their respective followers. But still, these kings reign for a time in their particular environment and eventually fade away like all other kings, and what remains is their name written and imprinted in history.

As long as planet Earth exists, kings will come and go, and all would have one thing in common: that their reign is limited for a time period, only in this world. But, as long as the planet exists, and indeed beyond that time, there will be only one King who will reign forever. This King will reign all over the entire Earth, will reign without limitations of time and borders, will reign forever and beyond the universe.

This King is the King of the peripheries.

Thank you for making time to read this book.

George Calleja (Christian Author)

Chapter One – Earthly kings vs The King

Earthly kings

Earthly kings are known to have conquered different parts of the world. History and even this present age can recount stories of different kings, stories that illustrate the kingdoms of this earth. The most common image that comes to our minds is a king with a crown, being a powerful person who conquers land, getting involved in battles to claim and protect his people's lands. Stories are told of kings being protected by thousands of soldiers, ready to die and risk their lives for their king, for the sake of the kingdom.

History books from all over the world name many different kings who ruled during a particular period. This book is not intended to go into the merit of who has been the greatest king who ever ruled the world, and neither will this book go into the merits of each king. Of course, it is still significant to mention a few of these kings, namely: King Tutankhamun (1341-23 BC), Cyrus The Great (580-529 BC), Alexander The Great (356-323 BC), King Augustus Caesar (63 BC-14 AD), King Henry VIII of England (1491-1547), Suleiman The Magnificent (1494-1566), King Louis XIV of France (1638-1715) and Frederick II of Prussia (1712-1786).

These kings, together with many others, are remembered for their achievements. Achievements of glory, of defeat, of power, of richness, of popularity, of changing and making the history of the world.

The King

With reference to the King, this book will concentrate on The King of the peripheries. So, who is this King of the peripheries, who is above all other earthly kings? This King is Jesus.

One of the very important episodes of the life of Jesus, who is the King, is highlighted in John 18:37 when Pilate asked Jesus *'You are a king, then!'* Jesus answered, *'You say that I am a king. In fact, the reason I was born and came into the world is to testify to the truth. Everyone on the side of truth listens to me.'* This short conversation between Pilate and Jesus carries a lot of importance.

To start with, Pontius Pilate, who arrived in Judea in AD 26, was likely a Roman knight who become famous through his military service. Pilate, as governor, had very important responsibilities at that time, mainly to keep law and order. It was a norm for Pilate, to visit Jerusalem during Jewish feasts and make sure that peace was kept in the city. Although not a king himself, Pilate knew who the kings of his time were, and who of them was the most powerful and the one to fear.

I have always wondered what Pilate meant exactly when he said to Jesus *'You are a king, then!'*. Why did Pilate make this statement? The fact that Pilate exclaimed such a straightforward statement, shows that Pilate ultimately did not have any doubt that Jesus spoke the truth, that Jesus was a King and that He had not committed any crime. This episode shows that Pilate, although in his heart knew who Jesus was, chose to reject Jesus. The decision that Pilate took of rejecting Jesus, is a tragedy, a tragedy that still occurs today. Whenever mankind rejects Jesus, mankind is being just another Pilate, the tragedy of recognising the truth but rejecting it.

In Jesus' reply to Pilate, *'You say that I am a king. In fact, the reason I was born and came into the world is to testify to the truth. Everyone on the side of truth listens to me'*, we notice that Jesus is aware that the people, as well as Pilate, think of Him as a King. Jesus reminds Pilate that He came to the world to bring the Truth, and that in fact, He was the Truth. Furthermore, Jesus also showed Pilate that those who do not reject Him, listen to Him. Jesus, in a loving way, showed Pilate that he was still rejecting Him, choosing not to listen to Him.

This episode in the life of Jesus, reminds me of what Pope Francis said in October 2020 during one of his addresses to the pilgrims gathered at St. Peter's Square at the Vatican. On this occasion Pope Francis reflected upon God's plan of salvation for humanity with regards to the day's Gospel reading (Matthew 22:1-14), where Jesus recounts a parable in which a king hosts a marriage feast for his son. During his reflection the Pope said that many of the originally invited guests refused to show up for the feast, and in his own words the Pope continued by saying that *"So often we too put our interests and material things ahead of the Lord who calls us."* Furthermore, the Pope explained, that the king persists in his desire to share the gifts of his kingdom, ordering his servants to go to the *"limits of the roads"* to invite whomever they find. The Pope further said that *"This is how God reacts: when He is rejected, rather than giving up, He starts over and asks that all those found at the thoroughfares be called, excluding no one."*

This is who the King is. This is the King of the peripheries. The King whose kingdom is not of this world, limited only to a specific land and territory, but a Kingdom where there is glory for all those who follow Him, for all those at the peripheries who accept Him, without limits of space and time. For in John 18:36, Jesus said to Pilate, *'My kingdom is not of this world. If it were, my servants would fight to prevent my arrest by the Jewish leaders. But now my kingdom is from another place.'* The Kingdom of Jesus is not of this world, and so the aim of our life is to not belong to this world, but to reach the ultimate goal of His Kingdom in Heaven.

Chapter Two – Who is in the peripheries and what are peripheries?

The crossroad that the Church is in

A couple of days before the conclave that elected Pope Francis in 2013, it is said that the Pope expressed himself to the cardinals that *'The church is called to come out of herself and to go to the peripheries, not only geographically, but also the existential peripheries: the mystery of sin, of pain, of injustice, of ignorance and indifference to religion, of intellectual currents and of all misery.'* Pope Francis could not have explained it much better than he did that day. Precisely, this is the crossroad that the Church is in, in today's history of society. This is where each member of the Church, each parish, each Christian group, and any other member of the Church, is to focus and reach out to.

Sin, pain, injustice, ignorance, indifferences to religion, intellectual currents, and misery, are what people all over the world are suffering from daily. Each one of these sufferings reflects a burden of life, a cross to live with, a cross that truly has already been carried by Jesus for the Salvation of mankind. Through His constant love for mankind, through the grace of the Trinity, the daily cross of mankind is continuously carried spiritually by Jesus.

Today's society is faced, amongst others, with conflicts involving military forces, with the never-ending problem of the refugee crisis, the constant challenges of oppression, the addiction to drugs, the increasing problem of human trafficking and child slavery, the range of poverty found not only in poor suburbs and so called third world countries, but also in wealthy cities and countries. This is just the tip of the iceberg of the plagues of society today. These are some of the most common issues mankind faces in our lifetime. This is what the peripheries are partly all about. People from different nations, cultures, races, and religions are present in these peripheries. These people are suffering from the lack of love, lack of injustice, lack of compassion, are suffering due to the darkness of evil.

This is the crossroad the Church is in, to reach out more to those in the peripheries.

Human rights and human dignity

In today's world we often hear about human rights and human dignity. Most of the news items we watch on social media treat the subject of human rights and human dignity constantly. But what is, in simple terms, the meaning of human rights and human dignity?

The United Nations defines human rights as follows: *'Human rights are rights we have simply because we exist as human beings - they are not granted by any state. These universal rights are inherent to us all, regardless of nationality, sex, national or ethnic origin, colour, religion, language, or any other status. They range from the most fundamental - the right to life - to those that make life worth living, such as the rights to food, education, work, health, and liberty.'* This book will not go into the issue if such human rights are truly safeguarded by all nations or if not, why.

It is worth keeping in mind, however, that millions of people still find it hard to have food to eat, and especially to have healthy and nutritious food to eat. This world still finds it hard to provide the proper education for our children, youths, and ongoing education to adults. Unemployment is still a big issue all over the world, bringing social problems and mental issues to the unemployed and their families. We can still see how the health system especially within the third world countries is not up to a standard, causing millions of people to get sick, and eventually die at a young age, forgotten by all. Freedom is still problematic in countries controlled by non-democratic governments. In some countries, the rights of human beings are still a long way to go. Such lack of human rights places these human beings in the peripheries of society, in the darkest alleys of life.

Now when one refers to human dignity, the Catechism of the Catholic Church (paragraph 356) defines human dignity as follows: *Of all visible creatures only man is "able to know and love his creator." He is "the only creature on earth that God has willed for its own sake," and he alone is called to share, by knowledge and love, in God's own life. It was for this end that he was created, and this is the fundamental reason for his dignity.* This is precisely what human dignity is all about, that is, to know and to love the creator, that is God. This is the difference between a human being and other creatures. Human beings were created to know God in a personal way and above all to love God the creator. No other creature can do this. The dignity of human beings is to know God and to love God, to be able to have this personal relationship with God.

The Catechism of the Catholic Church (paragraph 357) further elaborates on human dignity with more clarity as follows: *Being in the image of God, the human individual possesses the dignity of a person, who is not just something, but someone. He is capable of self-knowledge, of self-possession and of freely giving himself and entering into communion with other persons. And he is called by grace to a covenant with his Creator, to offer him a response of faith and love that no other creature can give in his stead.* A human being is not an object, or some modern art item. A human being is someone, is a person in the image of God. This is what human dignity is all about. It is about a person, called by grace to a covenant with his Creator, with God.

Who is in the peripheries and where are they?

In October 2018, the auxiliary bishop of Chicago, Bishop Joseph Perry, during his speech at the annual Missouri Catholic Conference General Assembly, explained very well who those in the peripheries are. In his words, based on the catechesis of Pope Francis, the peripheries include people who are ignored by hierarchical and governmental systems, as well as those who are illiterate or judged by their race or condition in life, immigrants, and refugees, the imprisoned, those who publicly sin, the elderly, sick and unborn.

We know who our brothers in the peripheries are, and where to find them. Different societies, towns, villages, and cities include also people living in the peripheries. It is a known fact that even in certain big corporations and businesses, one can find people who, although wealthy and rich, also form part of these peripheries. Their greed for money, and lack of values, create a vacuum in their spiritual life, as a result of which, their business actions are disconnected from God. This, in turn, often brings with it suffering to other people's lives.

It is also a known fact that certain places of entertainment are a beehive for drugs, prostitution, and human trafficking. Such places are not only frequented by youths and teenagers, but also adults and elderly people. These places are also known for gambling and money laundering, with many victims falling into this trap.

These are just a couple of examples of today's peripheries. One must not forget other peripheries, such as the prisons, hospitals, homeless people living in their cars, in a garage with lack of adequate sanitation, under a bridge or in card boxes, unwanted children living in institutions, and the list goes on.

Mother Teresa, a great example who reached out to the people in the peripheries

Saint Teresa of Calcutta, or as famously known, Mother Teresa, is surely one of today's great examples of people who, throughout their life, have reached out to people in the peripheries. Mother Teresa dedicated her whole life to be with, to live with, to comfort, to feed, to clothe and to carry out acts of love, with the poorest of the poor in India. Her experience of sharing and devoting her life to the poorest people, of being in the peripheries of Calcutta, was only possible through her personal relationship with Jesus. Even though she went through a spiritual darkness and suffered from a spiritual pain in her life, God still gave her the grace to be spiritually strong and be His light to the people in the peripheries, not only to those of Calcutta, but also to those various people she met throughout her missionary journeys.

Mother Teresa's experience is a strong spiritual witness of how she listened to the voice of God and reached out to the people in the peripheries. Her experience is a living testimony even today, after her death, as the order that she founded, the Missionaries of Charity, carries on her work up to this day. What Mother Teresa did in her life, she did it for Jesus - the King of the peripheries.

During the years 1990 to 1996, I twice had the privilege to be on some missionary experience helping the Missionaries of Charity, during my time as a missionary with *'The International Catholic*

Programme for Evangelization - ICPE'. In both these occasions, once in Albania and the other in Ghana, as ICPE we had spent a couple of days helping the Missionaries of Charity in their work. We spent our time with children with disabilities, playing with them, comforting them, trying to bring a smile on their faces and feeding them. These children were truly in the peripheries of their society, forgotten by all, abandoned, but lovingly taken care of by the dedicated sisters of the Missionaries of Charity. It was an experience I will always treasure my whole life, one of being with these angels, loving them and receiving their reciprocal love through their smile of happiness.

Chapter Three – The King of the peripheries

The King in the Gospels

Upon reading the Gospels, one will come across the words *'King'* or *'Kingdom'* on a number of occasions. This is not a surprise, when one considers that the message of the New Testament is based on the theme of the Kingdom of God. Going through some of the Gospels' verses that include the words *'King'* or *'Kingdom'*, amongst others, one will come up with the verses that follow. These verses are accompanied by a short reflection of mine, depicting in a short way the King of the peripheries.

Matthew 4:23 – 'Jesus went throughout Galilee, teaching in their synagogues, proclaiming the good news of the kingdom, and healing every disease and sickness among the people.' This particular verse from the Gospel of Matthew, clearly illustrates the three main aspects of the ministry of Jesus. These are teaching, so that there would be the understanding of the good news of the kingdom, preaching, which shows the concern of Jesus for commitment towards God, and healing, which brings wholeness to all. His miracles of healing prove his teachings and preaching and proves that he truly was from God.

Matthew 5:3 - 'Blessed are the poor in spirit, for theirs is the kingdom of heaven.' As is written in my book *'The Beatitudes... the blessings from the Sermon on the Mount'*, with regards to this verse from the Gospel of Matthew, to be poor in spirit is to become nothing, knowing that you totally depend upon God. The person who is poor in spirit, recognizes his smallness in front of God, and recognizes that God is everything in his life. Upon recognizing our sins, our weaknesses, recognizing that Christ is the Saviour... the gift of salvation is ours. It is at this point in our faith that the kingdom of heaven already becomes ours, even as from here on earth. The kingdom of heaven is the gift of salvation. It is the gift for all who are poor in spirit. This gift was brought to us by the loving act of Jesus... that of dying on the cross for our sins.

Matthew 5:10 - 'Blessed are those who are persecuted because of righteousness, for theirs is the kingdom of heaven.' Also, in my book *'The Beatitudes... the blessings from the Sermon on the Mount'*, I reflect upon how the eighth Beatitude speaks precisely that all those who in their lives are persecuted for living up to the truth, will be blessed for being righteous. It is a reality that keeps happening around us, that Christians are persecuted and face different sufferings for being faithful to the Truth. The blessing that Jesus preached in this Beatitude is that people who face persecution and suffering for their faith, will receive the kingdom of heaven as their own. This is the reward for these people, for all those who suffer persecution: they will receive the eternal reward of the kingdom of heaven.

Mark 10:14 - 'When Jesus saw this, he was indignant. He said to them, "Let the little children come to me, and do not hinder them, for the kingdom of God belongs to such as these.' Through this verse from the Gospel of Mark, Jesus clearly rebukes those who obstruct children from getting to know the Truth or from living the Truth, that is Jesus. Through this episode Jesus clearly shows that the Kingdom of God belongs to such children who suffer in some way or another from being denied knowing the Truth or are unable to live by it due to unfortunate circumstances they find themselves in.

Luke 9:11 - '...but the crowds learned about it and followed him. He welcomed them and spoke to them about the kingdom of God, and healed those who needed healing.' In this particular verse from the Gospel of Luke, Jesus makes it clear that the Kingdom of God belongs to everyone. Jesus knew that in the crowd that was gathered, not all believed in Him, that amongst the crowd many were just curious about Him or not grieving about their sins, but Jesus, through His compassion, still healed all the needy. Through these miracles Jesus made the Kingdom of God known to all those present, giving them the appropriate opportunity to believe in His Kingdom.

Luke 10:9 - 'Heal the sick who are there and tell them, 'The kingdom of God has come near to you.'' Reflecting upon this verse, also from the Gospel of Luke, clearly shows the need to reach out to all, to reach out to those who are excluded in society, to reach out to the peripheries. Jesus told His appointed seventy-two disciples not only to heal the sick, but more importantly to tell whoever they meet about the Kingdom of God, to teach the people about the King and bring hope to them. The teachings which Jesus asked the seventy-two disciples to bring forth to the people was of God's Love for them, of the new way of living, that is, of loving one's neighbour and of recognising that the Kingdom, His Love, is near.

Luke 12:32 - "Do not be afraid, little flock, for your Father has been pleased to give you the kingdom.' With reference to this particular verse from the Gospel of Luke, one clearly sees that all those living in the peripheries of society, are not to be afraid. The Love that the Father has for these people in the peripheries is immense. In return for their belief and trust in the Father, He will present to them His Kingdom. Salvation is also for these people living in the peripheries.

John 1:49 - 'Then Nathanael declared, "Rabbi, you are the Son of God; you are the king of Israel."' This particular episode from the Gospel of John, highlights Nathanael's conviction when declaring that Jesus is the King. What is interesting in this episode is that Nathanael replied to Jesus with these words upon being called as an apostle. Nathanael's faith in Jesus was very strong after the first words Jesus said to him, *'Here truly is an Israelite in whom there is no deceit',* as highlighted in John 1:47. Jesus' words to Nathanael were enough for him to convince himself and recognise that Jesus is the King.

John 3:3 - 'Jesus replied, "Very truly I tell you, no one can see the kingdom of God unless they are born again."' Another interesting episode about the Kingdom of God is illustrated in the Gospel of John 3:3. Here is the meeting between a Pharisee called Nicodemus who was a member of the Jewish ruling council, and Jesus. Nicodemus asked Jesus, as indicated in John 3:2 *'Rabbi, we know that you are a teacher who has come from God. For no one could perform the signs you are doing if God were not with him.'* In anticipation, Jesus interrupts Nicodemus and clearly replies *'Very truly I tell you, no one can see the kingdom of God unless they are born again.'* The answer of Jesus to Nicodemus implies the importance for a person to experience a thorough change in heart and in life. This change through divine grace is necessary not only for Nicodemus and the other members of the Jewish ruling council, but for all mankind. It is through this change of heart and life, of this *'second birth'* that one may truly recognise and see the Kingdom of God.

John 12:15 - "Do not be afraid, Daughter Zion; see, your king is coming, seated on a donkey's colt." This particularly interesting episode as narrated in the Gospel of John 12:15, took place when Jesus entered Jerusalem. Here Jesus quotes from Zechariah 9:9, declaring Himself as coming into Jerusalem in peace and not for war. Jesus, through this episode declared that He is the King. Jesus knew that the real truth of His Kingdom, would only be evident at the crucifixion which was to follow.

These quotations taken from the Gospels together with the related reflections, portray in a small way the powerful words of *'King'* or *'Kingdom'* with reference to Jesus. Surely these quotations from the Gospels truly portray Jesus as the King of all and the true only King, not of this world, but of the coming Kingdom.

My insight about the King of the peripheries

On the 21 November 2020, I was on a day visit to the sister island of Malta, called Gozo. It was a day to treat myself for a short break from the hectic daily life. I spent most of the day visiting some historical places in Gozo, taking it easy and spending some time of reflection upon life. In the evening I went for the 6.00pm mass at the National Shrine of the Blessed Virgin of Ta' Pinu.

During mass I felt inspired about what Christian book I should write next. The theme of *'King of the peripheries'* was stirring deeply in my heart and mind. The more time went by during mass, the more I was at peace with it. I could understand more, in a new way, that Jesus is the *'King of the peripheries'*, the King who goes all the way to bring peace, love, healing to the prisoners, the poor, the sick, to the families throughout the world.

I could understand more, how important it is for all Christians to visit and be with these people who suffer alone in the different peripheries of society, and above all to see Jesus in them. In my insight, I could understand that God will judge us not because we visit these people, but because we see Jesus in these people. In other words, God will judge us for recognising Jesus in these people and for visiting Jesus through these people, bringing them His Love. This is how God will judge us.

It is very important to be aware that we are not to judge these people, but we are to serve them by seeing Jesus in them. God wants us all to be another Jesus for these people in the peripheries and bring Jesus to them in their life.

As the homily of the mass was based on Christ the King, I could understand more that Christians need to recognise the King in the poor and the needy. This is where Christ the King is present: in the poor, as Christ is not a king of the world as we understand of a worldly king, but He is the King in the poor person, in the sick person, the prisoners etc. In other words, it is there that Christ the King is to be found, it is there that He is present in today's society: He is in the peripheries.

As Christians, we are to recognise Him by being with these people in the peripheries, and our attitude is not to be that of feeling good or holy for having visited and helped these people, but we should feel humbled for having recognised Christ the King in them. We need to keep in mind that Christ the King is in each person living in the peripheries, living in broken circumstances and situations that society brings these people to.

Chapter Four – Called to reach out to the peripheries

Bring the Gospel to the needy

In 2018, as already mentioned, one of the keynote speakers at the annual Missouri Catholic Conference General Assembly, Bishop Perry, emphasised to the congregation, the importance for Catholics to bring the Gospel to the people in need. Bishop Perry was bringing forth the message that Pope Francis set to all Catholics, that to bring the Gospel to the people in need, requires both to go out to all nations and of utter importance to bring the Gospel in an existential world through a person's experience of pain, through an experience of suffering and indifferences.

Bishop Perry further emphasised that the peripheries include people who are ignored in society. Here Bishop Perry referred to those people being ignored due to hierarchical and governmental systems, to those being ignored due to being illiterate, or to those being judged by their race and condition in life. According to Bishop Perry, people in the peripheries are the immigrants and refugees, the imprisoned, the elderly, the sick, the unborn and also those who publicly sin. Bishop Perry also noted that all these people in the peripheries, and more, have become the important matter in today's catechesis of this papacy.

I believe that Bishop Perry could not have explained it better. This message, although addressed to Catholics gathered during a

Catholic Conference General Assembly, was also a message for all Christians of whatever church and denomination they belong to, and to all people of good will. The needy people in the peripheries are made up of people of different race, different colour, different religion, and all need to be reached through the Gospel, through different acts of love that these people require and are yearning for.

People yearn to be loved

Throughout my experience of life, especially after I accepted God's love for me, I can tell how much people yearn for love. I have witnessed this yearning for love first-hand through various encounters. These occasions of evangelising different people from various cultures and religions, various ages and race, have strengthened my faith through witnessing people accepting the love of Jesus in their life.

It has always been a strong experience to witness people in the peripheries: prisoners, drug addicts, sick people, orphans and especially people with a lack of faith, to come and recognise God in their life. These people, whom I have encountered over a number of years, carried within them this yearning to be loved, to be loved by God, to know that He loves them, to accept Him in their lives. It has always been a privilege and spiritually uplifting for me to see the smile on their face, to see them weep with joy, to hear their *'thank you'*, for being comforted by Him even though they were in the peripheries.

These experiences which I have gone through in Albania, Germany, Ghana, Holland, Malta, Poland, Romania, Russia and Tunisia amongst others, and which I still experience today in my own country, have been and are spiritual treasures. People in the peripheries are found in every corner of the world, waiting to be reached, to be fed, to be clothed, to receive the word of God and become strong in their faith and follow Him.

People in the peripheries deserve, and are worthy, to be reached out to and receive His love.

For I was hungry and you gave me something to eat

The importance of going out and reaching out to the people in the peripheries should be a priority in the daily life of every Christian. We are to go out and literally search for the poor in our society, in our environment, in our workplace, in every possible place that these people may be found. This requires that we go out of our own comfort zones and be ready and get our hands and feet dirty, to sacrifice our time for them and rejoice in being with them. Christians are to go out to relate to these people in the peripheries, to be their friend and to serve them, to be humble and be just like Jesus to them.

It is only by being Jesus to their neighbour that Christians would really be honouring Jesus, witnessing that He is the King of all people all over the world, that He is the King of the peripheries. In this way the poor person in the periphery can recognise Christ, accept Him and truly celebrate that Christ is the King of the universe.

As is narrated in Matthew 25:31-43 *"When the Son of Man comes in his glory, and all the angels with him, he will sit on his glorious throne. All the nations will be gathered before him, and he will separate the people one from another as a shepherd separates the sheep from the goats. He will put the sheep on his right and the goats on his left.*

"Then the King will say to those on his right, 'Come, you who are blessed by my Father; take your inheritance, the kingdom prepared for you since the creation of the world. For I was hungry and you gave me something to eat, I was thirsty and you gave me something to drink, I was a stranger and you invited me in, I needed clothes and you clothed me, I was sick and you looked after me, I was in prison and you came to visit me.'

"Then the righteous will answer him, 'Lord, when did we see you hungry and feed you, or thirsty and give you something to drink? When did we see you a stranger and invite you in, or needing clothes and clothe you? When did we see you sick or in prison and go to visit you?'

"The King will reply, 'Truly I tell you, whatever you did for one of the least of these brothers and sisters of mine, you did for me.'

"Then he will say to those on his left, 'Depart from me, you who are cursed, into the eternal fire prepared for the devil and his angels. For I was hungry and you gave me nothing to eat, I was thirsty and you gave me nothing to drink, I was a stranger and you did not invite me in, I needed clothes and you did not clothe me, I was sick and in prison and you did not look after me.'*

This is who Christ the King is. This is why we are to reach out to the people in the peripheries. Jesus healed the marginalised, comforted the marginalised, brought hope to the marginalised, so that they, the marginalised, will also be in His Kingdom, because He is the King of the peripheries.

About the Author

George Calleja grew up in Malta and is married with two children. In 2009 he obtained his MBA through the University of Leicester.

During the years 1990 to 1996 he was a full-time missionary with *'The International Catholic Programme for Evangelization - ICPE'* and evangelised in various countries such as Russia, Ghana, Poland, Germany, and Malta amongst others. Since 1997, he has been an active member of the Focolare Movement in Malta.

In 2012 George embarked on a mission of evangelisation through the use of various social media. His first Christian book *'Peace and Unity in our lives – Volume One'* was published in November 2014. Since then, he has published another 15 Christian books focusing on various themes. His writings are also published in various other Christian social media, such as *Laikos* and *Catholic365.com*.

Being a dedicated Christian writer, George Calleja is actively involved in spreading the Good News through various means on social media. His writings on blogs and various prominent websites, together with his podcasts and videos, make him an example of how to evangelise in today's society through technology.

His latest evangelisation project is that of providing online Christian courses, namely *'Living the Beatitudes in your life'*, *'How to heal your spiritual wounds'* and' *Getting to know about Mary's silence'*, all available through Udemy. Furthermore, George Calleja has also embarked to evangelise through his YouTube Channel with his Christian programme *'God Loves You'*.

Connect with the Author

If you would like to contact the author, please email him at:

peacethroughunity@gmail.com

You can also follow him through the following social links:-

Blog:

http://peacethroughunity.blogspot.com/

FaceBook:

https://www.facebook.com/georgecallejaebooks/timeline

GoodReads:

https://www.goodreads.com/author/show/9847194.George_Calleja

Instagram:

https://www.instagram.com/george_calleja_author/

Smashwords:

https://www.smashwords.com/profile/view/geocalpeace

Spotify:

https://open.spotify.com/show/6xDW2laQcnWtRBAmpjT39D

Twitter:

https://twitter.com/PeaceUnityLives

Udemy:

https://www.udemy.com/user/george-calleja/

Website:

https://sites.google.com/site/peaceinunity/

WordPress:

http://peacethroughunity.wordpress.com/

YouTube Channel:

https://www.youtube.com/channel/UCkS4BJLIeodVZAS8i6Sn6Og

Future books to be published

Writing Christian books is a passion in the life of the author. His passion is that of seeking to bring peace to the world, to make it a better place to live in and to draw people closer to God. As a Catholic, it has become his mission to share the love of God through his writings. The joy of sharing the love of God with the reader is tremendous and it uplifts his life and also that of his family.

For these reasons, the author is always planning ahead about what to write next. By late 2022, George Calleja will be publishing another Christian book which you are encouraged to look out for.

For further information about his publications, please visit his FaceBook page at:

https://www.facebook.com/georgecallejaebooks/timeline

or visit the authors official website 'George Calleja – Christian Author' at:

https://sites.google.com/site/georgecallejachristianauthor/

Published books

'Emmaus... in today's society'

Published: 26 November 2020

ISBN: 9781005477639

'Come To Me'

Published: 29 September 2019

ISBN: 9780463950067

'Her Silence'

Published: 12 January 2019

ISBN: 9780463348161

'In His Image'

Published: 17 June 2018

ISBN: 9780463849132

'Spiritual Reflections'

Published: 17 December 2017

ISBN: 9781370553839

'Waking up the sleeping giant'

Published: 30 July 2017

ISBN: 9781370926558

'Heal my Wounds'

Published: 26 February 2017

ISBN: 9781370423712

'The Light'

Published: 30 September 2016

ISBN: 9781370445110

'Taste and see that the Lord is good'

Published: 17 April 2016

ISBN: 9781310361579

'My Little Book Of Daily Prayer'

Published: 10 January 2016

ISBN: 9781311849472

'The Beatitudes... The Blessings From The Sermon On the Mount'

Published: 27 September 2015

ISBN: 9781311169006

'Evangelization Through Social Networking Sites'

Published: 14 June 2015

ISBN: 9781310647598

'Yes... I will follow Him'

Published: 8 March 2015

ISBN: 9781310576287

'Peace and Unity in our lives – Volume Two'

Published: 21 January 2015

ISBN: 9781310758577

'Peace and Unity in our lives – Volume One'

Published: 9 November 2014

ISBN: 9781310773280

While thanking you for reading 'The King... of the peripheries', I hope that it has helped you to increase your faith and to draw you closer to God. As an independent author, the success of my books relies mostly on reviews and recommendations by readers such as yourself. If you found this book useful, please tell others about it... your family, your friends etc. I highly appreciate your assistance to share about this book and to share about God's love.

Thank you and God bless you!

George Calleja (Christian Author)